Wonders of
Alligators
and
Crocodiles

by WYATT BLASSINGAME

Illustrated with photographs

SCHOLASTIC BOOK SERVICES
NEW YORK · TORONTO · LONDON · AUCKLAND · SYDNEY · TOKYO

For Laura Hempstead Jackson
who as a very small girl
prayed the whales would
not eat all the alligators

Picture credits: Bruce Coleman Inc./M. Turnauckas: 14 (bottom). Florida Game & Fresh Water Fish Commission: Mike Fogerty 39; Wallace Hughes 38, 40, 46, 52, 55, 84; Larry Martin 35 (right); Gene Smith 10 (bottom), 18, 49, 57, 60, 83; Lovett Williams 93. Florida News Bureau, Department of Commerce: cover, 10 (top left), 12 (top), 14, 24, 30, 64, 67. Kenya Information Services: 73. Ministry of Information, Salisbury, Rhodesia: 7, 71, 75, 78, back cover. Mozert Studios, Silver Springs, Florida: 12 (bottom), 91. National Park Service, United States Department of the Interior: 22, 43; John C. Ogden 35 (left), 42. Ross Allen Reptile Institute: 10 (top right), 68, 86-87. South African Tourist Corporation: 80.

2nd printing . . . . February 1974
Printed in the U.S.A.

Author's Note

My personal acquaintance with alligators and crocodiles has largely been limited to research and some rather wary watching over a number of years. For their help with this book, I'd like to express my appreciation to several persons who have been associated with these crocodilians far more closely than I have:

Mr. Ross Allen of the Reptile Institute, Silver Springs, Florida; Lester and Bill Piper at the Everglades Wonder Gardens, Bonita Springs, Florida; Dr. John Ogden at the Everglades National Park; Bill Hansen and Wallace Hughes of the *Florida Wildlife Magazine*.

I am also very much indebted to Mr. Wilfred T. Neill, from whose excellent book, *The Last of the Ruling Reptiles*, Columbia University Press, I have gathered much information.

Many thanks.

Contents

From the Time
of the Dinosaurs

Ancient travelers along the Nile River in Egypt often heard a noise that sounded like children weeping. When they hurried to offer help, they found the noise was made by huge crocodiles. And the crocodiles, still weeping false tears, quickly ate their would-be helpers. At least, that's the legend, and it explains how the expression "crocodile tears," meaning a hypocritical pretense of sorrow, came into being. But don't you believe it.

Possibly no other animals have been the source of so many untrue stories as alligators and crocodiles. Even people who ought to know better talk about monsters 40 feet long and 500 years old, blowing great clouds of smoke from their nostrils when they bellow. But no living person ever saw an alligator or crocodile 40 feet long. They only live 50 or 60 years, at the most. Even though they look like dragons, they don't blow smoke from their nostrils. And certainly they don't make sounds like weeping children.

However, it is easy to understand how these wild stories came into being. Crocodilians have fascinated people for thousands of years. (Crocodiles and alligators are not the same, but the word "crocodilian" does refer to both, as well as to their other close relatives.) Yet in all that time, little was truly known about them. Even today, scientists are just beginning to study them carefully and much is still unknown.

A crocodile at the Wankie Game Reserve in Rhodesia.

During the time that scientists call the Cretaceous Period, gigantic reptiles dominated the earth. This was from about 135 million years ago to about 63 million years ago. There were flesh-eating dinosaurs 50 feet long, with terrible knifelike teeth. There were dinosaurs with horns, and something called *Brontosaurus* that might have weighed 30 tons. There were giant, lizardlike birds with leathery wings. And there were crocodilians.

Some of these early crocodilians got into the spirit of the time and grew to be monsters. Some had horns, and some actually were 50 feet long. But there were also alligators and crocodiles exactly like those we have today.

Then came the end of what has been called the Age of Ruling Reptiles. For some unknown reason, the dinosaurs disappeared. The lizardlike birds, the 50-foot alligators, vanished. But the crocodilians we have today survived, among the most ancient of all living creatures.

The Kinds of Crocodilians and How to Tell Them Apart

Scientists divide these surviving crocodilians into four large groups. These are: crocodiles, alligators, caimans, and gavials — or gharials, since it is spelled both ways. These four groups are further divided into smaller ones. There are 14 species of crocodiles, two of alligators, five caimans, and two gavials. Some naturalists say that one of the gavials should be called Tomistoma rather than gavial, but the differences are too small for most of us to worry about. Indeed, many of these various species are so much alike that only an expert can tell them apart. There are, however, some obvious differences between the large family groups. Take, for example, the coloring.

Alligators are mostly black, with yellowish lines and spots. Crocodiles are more gray, with black spots. Caimans are a sort of dirty tan, with dark spots and bands across the body and tail. The color of gavials is much like that of caimans, with widely spaced dark bands.

9

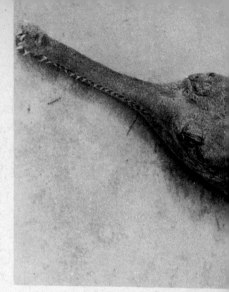

ABOVE: The gavial's snout is so long and narrow that it has been said to look like "the handle on a frying pan."

LEFT: The alligator can be distinguished by its broad, rounded snout.

The caiman's snout is slightly more pointed than that of the alligator.

All these color differences are much more noticeable in the babies than in the adults. As any crocodilian gets older, the markings on its body begin to fade. The easiest way to tell the adults of the four groups apart is by the shape of the head.

The alligator has a broad, rounded snout. The caiman's snout is slightly more pointed than that of the alligator. And one species, called the spectacled caiman, has a raised, bony ridge just in front of the eyes. Some people call these eyebrowed caimans. Imported from Central America, they are sometimes sold in pet shops as baby alligators.

The crocodile's snout is long and tapered, coming to a narrower point than that of the caiman which, in turn, is narrower than the broad snout of the alligators. And the gavial's snout is so long and so narrow it can't possibly be mistaken for any of the others. Some people say it looks like the handle on a frying pan.

There is another way in which the alligator and crocodile may sometimes be told apart. With their mouths open, both may look as if they had 5,000 teeth, all cone-shaped, long, and pointed. Actually, the American crocodile has only 68 teeth, while the American alligator may have 80 or more. Nobody wants to count the teeth on a live alligator to tell it from a crocodile, but there's another method.

An alligator can be distinguished from a crocodile by the large fourth tooth in the lower jaw. In the alligator (above) that tooth does not show when the reptile's mouth is closed. In the crocodile (below), it does.

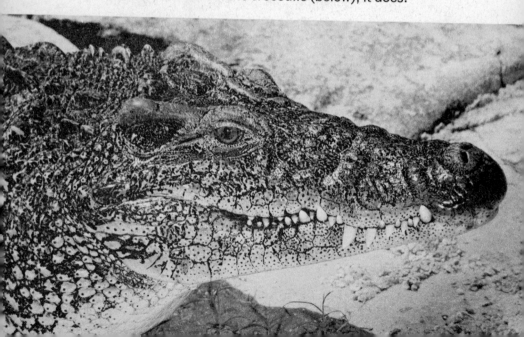

When the alligator's mouth is shut, the big fourth tooth from the front in the lower jaw fits into a cavity in the upper jaw, out of sight. Some of the 'gator's teeth may be visible, but not this one near the front. When the crocodile's mouth is shut, this fourth tooth in the lower jaw still shows.

Where crocodilians live

Like all reptiles, crocodilians are cold-blooded animals. This means that their bodies have no way of warming the blood. The body temperature, then, must always be the same, or near the same, as that of the area in which they live. Some reptiles do manage to live in places where the weather gets extremely cold. But crocodilians need both warmth and water. Given these, one species or another may be found over a large part of the tropical and semi-tropical world. They live along the coasts, the rivers, and swamps, in parts of South, Central, and North America, Africa, India, the East Indies, almost anywhere that it is both very warm and very wet.

The range of the individual species, however, is much more limited. Caimans are found only in Central and South America. Gavials live in India and on a few islands around the South China Sea.

One or more species of crocodile may be seen in

The American alligator (above) is mostly found in the swamplands of southern Georgia and Louisiana and many parts of Florida. The Chinese alligator (below) is found only in the Yangtze-Kiang river basin.

many parts of the tropical world. Only one, however, lives anywhere in the United States. This is the American crocodile, a very few of which live in Florida, along the southern edge of the Everglades.

Of the two kinds of alligators, one is found nowhere in the world except in the southeastern section of the United States. This is the alligator that most people know. Scientists call it *Alligator mississipiensis*, the second name being for the Mississippi River, near which many of the early specimens were seen. At one time, these alligators lived all the way from the southeastern corner of Virginia to the Florida Keys and around the Gulf of Mexico to the Rio Grande. Today, however, they are mostly found in the Okefenokee Swamp of southern Georgia, in many parts of Florida, and in southern Louisiana.

The other species of alligator, strangely enough, is found nowhere except in a very small area of China. Although it has lived there since long before the first man, not much is really known about it. No one even knows why the only two species in the world should be so widely separated. It was the Chinese 'gator that gave rise to the ancient stories of fire-breathing dragons, but it doesn't actually breathe any fire. In fact, it is rarely more than five feet long, much smaller than its American relative, and quite shy.

The American Alligator

In the sixteenth century Spanish explorers found what they thought were giant lizards crawling about the swamps of Florida, Cuba, and South America. Some of these were alligators, some were crocodiles; but the Spanish called them all *el lagarto*, which simply meant "the lizard." English-speaking people changed *el lagarto* to alligator. And so the American alligator obtained its name.

The first pictures we have of *el lagarto* were drawn by a French artist named Jacques Le Moyne, who voyaged to Florida in 1564. Most of the Frenchmen who came with Le Moyne were promptly murdered by the Spanish. The artist, however, escaped and returned to Europe. There, many years later, he began to paint from memory a number of the things he had seen in America. On the alligators, at least, his imagination must have been working overtime. He pictured them as huge monsters, 30 to 40 feet long.

Indians killed them, he said, by pushing a big log into the alligator's mouth so it could not bite, then attacking with clubs and arrows.

True, a few of the alligators in Le Moyne's day may have been a little bit bigger than any now living. Certainly, there were more of them. Almost nothing can harm an adult alligator except man. Although Indians sometimes hunted them for food, they did not kill many. So in the Florida swamps, and around the coast of the Gulf of Mexico, the 'gators thrived in large numbers.

William Bartram, a naturalist who explored Florida just before the American Revolution, described a scene on the St. Johns River. "The alligators," he wrote, "were in such incredible numbers and so close together from shore to shore, that it would have been easy to have walked across on their heads, had the animals been harmless."

With ample food and few enemies, some of these alligators must have lived to a ripe old age. Even so, it is doubtful if William Bartram — or even an American Indian — ever saw an alligator more than 19 or 20 feet long. Today, most scientists set the maximum size at about 18 feet. And the average grown 'gator is more likely to be 10 or 12 feet long.

The alligator's legs are extremely short in comparison with his body, but they can lift him clear of the ground. For a brief distance, he can move with amazing speed.

The 'gator in water and on land

The alligator, like all crocodilians, is amphibious — capable of living both on land and in the water. In fact, both land and water are necessary for them to survive.

On land, the alligator looks awkward. Compared to its tremendous body, its legs are extremely short, particularly the front ones. Resting, it usually lies flat, with all four legs flopped loosely at its sides. But when frightened or angry, those legs prove stronger than they look. They can lift the huge body clear off the ground, and, for a very short distance, the 'gator can move with surprising speed. But it tires quickly; its body sinks lower and drags. After a first rush of

20 to 30 feet, the 'gator moves so slowly that a man can easily outdistance it.

In water, the alligator is something else altogether. It has five toes on its front feet and four on its back feet; and these are webbed like a duck's. But it doesn't actually use its feet for swimming. If the water is very shallow, the 'gator may use them to half-walk, half-paddle. But where the water is deeper, the alligator holds its stubby legs against its sides and swims with sweeps of its mighty tail. Here its speed is truly amazing.

At rest in the water, the alligator looks like a half-sunken log. Usually, only the tip of the snout, the eyes, and a little bit of the back is showing. It can lie like this for hours, perfectly motionless, because it breathes through openings on the top and front of its snout. From here, the air does not go into its mouth. Instead, there is a narrow, enclosed passage that leads from the nose along the roof of the mouth to the throat.

Alligators catch most of their food near or under the water, so they need to be able to open their mouths underwater without swallowing half the pond in which they are swimming. This problem is solved by valves located in the alligator's nose and at the back of its mouth. When the alligator dives, these automatically close, like the hatch of a submarine.

Effects of temperature

Nobody is quite sure how long an alligator can stay underwater without breathing. Indeed, this depends on a number of different things. One of these is the temperature. All crocodilians, remember, are cold-blooded. Their body temperature is much the same as that of the surrounding air or water. Alligators can stand colder temperatures for longer periods of time than any other type of crocodilian because they are better at a kind of hibernation. As the weather turns cold in winter, the alligator becomes more and more sluggish. Its breathing gets slower. In the wild, the alligator will seek a cave of some kind, where it may stay for weeks or even months. With winter rains, the alligator's cave may fill, or almost fill, with water, and some people believe that, at this time, the alligator can go a month or more without breathing. Others believe there is always a little bit of air in the 'gator's cave, enough so that it can breathe now and then.

Temperature affects not only an alligator's breathing, but also its appetite. In cold weather, it may not eat for weeks, or even months. But men who raise them in captivity have learned there is an odd difference between those born in Georgia and South Carolina and those from southern Florida.

In captivity, an alligator may be placed in an

enclosed pen and kept at the same temperature the year round. But if it came from an area where, each year, the weather turns cold in winter, then the alligator will lose its appetite in winter, even if kept warm. On the other hand, at the Everglades Wonder Gardens, in southern Florida, alligators born in the glades just keep right on eating.

Effect of exercise

Besides the temperature, another thing that affects the alligator's breathing is the amount of exercise it takes. In warm weather, an alligator may lie motionless on the bottom for 10 to 20 minutes, rise unhurriedly to the surface, take a breath, and go down again. But if a school of fish passes and the alligator lashes about to catch them, it must surface more often. And if it is trapped and struggling, the alligator must breathe every few minutes.

Ross Allen, who runs the Reptile Institute at Silver Springs, Florida, once drowned an alligator by mistake. Allen was wrestling underwater with an eight-foot alligator as part of the show. At this time Allen had been working with crocodilians for only a few years and had no idea how long one could live without breathing. Several times during the act, Allen came to the surface for a quick breath, but held the alligator down. Suddenly the 'gator quit struggling.

When Allen brought it to the surface, it was dead — drowned. In his shows after this, Allen has never held an alligator underwater for more than one or two minutes at a time.

The 'gator's eye

Since the alligator takes much of its food underwater, it needs to be able not only to hold its breath, but also to see beneath the surface. In order to accomplish this, it has three eyelids. There is an upper

In addition to an upper and lower eyelid, the alligator has a third transparent lid, to keep out the water when it dives.

and lower lid. If the 'gator is just taking a nap, these lids slide together and shut out the light. But beneath this pair there is a third lid, thin and transparent. When the 'gator dives, the outside lids stay open, while the third lid slides over the eye to keep out the water, much like a skin diver's glass mask.

There is another odd thing about the alligator's eyes which nobody seems to understand. In the daylight, the pupil is not round like that of a human being. Instead, it is a narrow slot, like a buttonhole, straight up and down. If the alligator raises his head, the pupil is still straight up and down.

At night, the shape of the pupil appears to change. At least, when caught in a sudden bright light, the whole eye glows round and bright, ruby-red. Alligator hunters working at night use lights fastened to their caps. With these, they can spot the red glow of the 'gator's eyes when the rest of its body is underwater or hidden in the bushes.

The 'gator's teeth

An alligator's teeth are almost as odd as its eyes — at least from the human point of view. A man has only two sets of teeth — one as a small child, and one a little later, which must last for the rest of his life. But an alligator has many sets. When one tooth begins to wear out, another pushes up inside the cone of the old one and replaces it. Just how often this may happen, nobody really knows. But when an alligator gets very old, new teeth quit forming. A very old alligator may have almost no teeth at all.

The alligator's cone-shaped teeth are not made for grinding food but for tearing it into large chunks that

The alligator's teeth are not made for chewing, but for catching and holding.

may be swallowed. The actual breaking down of the food takes place in the alligator's stomach. Strong acids help with this breakdown. But there may be another and very curious aid.

For some unknown reason, alligators swallow hard objects. In the wild, a young alligator will swallow twigs and small pebbles. A bigger alligator will swallow bigger rocks and chunks of wood. In captivity, they will swallow coins, bottles, photographers' flashbulbs — just about anything that is thrown to them. Crocodiles also have this curious dining custom. A few years ago, a veterinarian operated on a crocodile in the Cincinnati Zoo. In its stomach he found six bottles, 39 rocks, three marbles, a porcelain elephant, two cartridge cases, and a metal whistle!

This strange habit has given rise to some equally strange theories. In ancient Egypt, people believed it was the crocodile's way of keeping count. Some said he swallowed a rock for every person he ate. Some said he swallowed one each year to keep up with his age.

Even today, naturalists disagree on the reason. A few believe the animal swallows heavy objects as ballast to help it float on a more level keel in the water. Some say the added weight helps the crocodilian to drag large prey, such as a deer or wild pig, into the water. Both of these reasons sound doubtful. Most naturalists believe the crocodilians use these hard objects to help grind the food in their stomachs.

Whatever the reason, alligators and crocodiles sometimes carry this strange appetite too far. Naturalists at Ross Allen's Reptile Institute have often studied the bodies of dead alligators. Some of the 'gators, they discovered, had swallowed enough hard objects to block the anal passage and cause death.

One of the strangest things about alligators also applies to some lizards and other reptiles. If you have a pet chameleon, you might try this experiment on it. When an alligator is turned on its back and held there, and its belly is rubbed, it will go to sleep or become unconscious. Nobody seems to know which, or why. Roll it back over and, after a few moments, it wakes up and goes about its business.

How dumb are alligators?

Some naturalists believe that, on its back, the alligator loses consciousness because of pressure on its small brain. And it is true that none of the crocodilians are very smart. But when it is a matter of survival, they can learn — and quickly!

In a wild area where alligators are frequently hunted, they learn to hide at the sight of a search-

light or the sound of a boat. In captivity, they learn
to recognize the voice of the man who feeds them.
If food is always brought in the same wheelbarrow,
they learn the special sound of that wheelbarrow.
When the 'gators hear it coming, they move forward,
ready to eat. But another wheelbarrow of the same
kind may pass without one of them opening a sleepy
eye.

Not long ago, a motion picture about the Seminole
War was being made in the Everglades. The director
wanted a scene in which the Indians pretended to
throw captive soldiers into a pit full of alligators. He
asked the Piper brothers at the Everglades Wonder
Gardens to furnish the alligators.

"We have plenty of alligators," Bill Piper said.
"But in captivity, 'gators get accustomed to being fed
in one place. Move them, and they may quit eating
for a while."

The director insisted, and the Pipers took a dozen
big alligators from the Wonder Gardens to a small
pond in the Everglades. While cameras photo-
graphed it all, the make-believe Indians, with loud
whoops and hollers, hurled dummy soldiers to the
alligators — and the alligators immediately dived to
the bottom of the pond to hide.

The director tried again, this time with chicken

blood smeared on the dummies to fool the alligators. It didn't work.

Finally, the alligators were taken back to the Gardens that they considered home. Tree limbs were put around their pen, to make it look like the wilderness. The dummies were stuffed, not with cloth but with fish on which the 'gators were used to being fed. Once more, the screaming Indians hurled them into the alligator pond.

The alligators tore into them. Boots and hats and bits of clothing flew in every direction. The water of the pond turned red with fish blood.

Later, the director decided not to use the scene. "It was too gruesome," he told Bill and Lester Piper. "But those alligators are not as dumb as I thought they were."

The Voice of the 'Gator

When an alligator bellows, it raises its head slightly. It keeps its mouth shut. And it blows out its breath in a series of long, rumbling roars that, on a quiet night, may be heard for half a mile or more. In a swamp, the bellow of a 'gator will actually set the earth itself to quivering. People have described it as sounding like thunder, like the voices of a thousand bullfrogs singing, and like the rumble of a passing freight train.

There is no doubt at all that alligators bellow, yet no one is sure of all the reasons why. Naturalists once believed that only the male bellowed, and that this was a challenge to other males. This belief probably came about because, in the wild, it is impossible to tell the male alligator from the female. It is now known that both sexes bellow, one just as loudly as the other.

In captivity, a whole pen full of alligators, lying peacefully side by side, may all start to bellow. Then they will all quit and go quietly to sleep again without ever having moved except to raise their heads.

Sounds often set alligators to roaring. Thunder or the noise of a passing airplane may start them off. Nor does the sound need to be a loud one. Several years ago this was proved by an unusual experiment at a museum of natural history.

Although this alligator may look as if it is bellowing, it is only waiting to be fed. The alligator keeps its mouth closed when bellowing.

An alligator named Oscar began to roar when a workman accidentally banged on some nearby steel rods. Noticing this, the scientists began to experiment. They found that, if the rods were strummed rapidly, Oscar paid no heed. But if the rods were strummed at five- to 10-second intervals, Oscar raised his head and bellowed.

Next, some musicians were brought to help with the experiment. At first, Oscar ignored them. But whenever a single instrument hit B-flat, Oscar's head reared up and he let go with what the museum called a "moderately loud, deep note that suddenly increased in volume and rose in very sharp crescendo."

Under normal conditions in the wild, each adult alligator, male and female, usually has its own territory. Of course, this may change with conditions. Drought may force a number of 'gators to gather around a single pond. A lack of food in some places and an abundance in another may bring them together. But normally the adults live apart. At such times, some naturalists believe, the alligator's bellow serves as a kind of love call. At least it may let one alligator know where the other one is.

Summing it up, Ross Allen says, "An alligator bellows about like a rooster crows or a man talks. It's his voice, and he uses it in different ways."

The voice of the crocodile

Crocodiles, particularly the American crocodile, are quiet creatures compared to alligators. The young of both species may make grunting noises, but alligators make them louder and more often. And where the adult alligator will not only bellow but also make loud hissing noises, the grown American crocodile is chiefly silent. Like the alligator, it can hiss as a warning, though. Sometimes it will make a soft coughing sound. But it does not bellow.

Courtship

Alligators go a-courting in the spring, usually in late March or early April. Just how old an alligator must be before it mates is uncertain. At Ross Allen's Reptile Institute, one female mated at the age of two and a half. Most, however, are about five or six years old and about five or six feet long, before they are sexually mature.

In the very early spring, the female appears to be more interested in finding a mate than the male. However, once she locates him, she quickly turns coy. It is the male that does the active courting. For two or three days, sometimes for two or three weeks, the male follows the female wherever she goes. If she goes swimming, he swims along behind her. If she crawls out on the bank, he follows. If she lies still, either in the water or on the bank, he will lie beside her. Then, with what seems to be a kind of love pat, he rubs her back with one of his feet. Sometimes the two alligators will lie facing one another in the water. The male puts his head under the female's head and bumps it gently, as if he were tickling her under the chin. After this, they may take turns blowing long streams of bubbles past one another's face.

In captivity, the male alligator courts one female only. This is probably true in the wild also. But after mating, the male loses interest and wanders away. About two months later, the female starts building her nest.

Nest building

Usually, the nest is very near the pond or creek in which the female makes her home. However, in places where there is an unusually large number of adults, there may be no babies or nests at all. Perhaps the female instinctively fears that, under these crowded conditions, other adults will eat her eggs or young, so she may travel a mile or more away to make her nest. This, however, is very rare.

Wherever the nest is built, it will be high enough above ground to avoid flooding. Also, it must be where the female can get the material with which to build. If there is not much suitable ground available, several females may build within a few yards of one another. Usually, however, the nests are far apart.

LEFT: The alligator makes its nest from the material available. This nest, in the Everglades National Park, is constructed chiefly of saw grass and dirt.

RIGHT: Alligator eggs are bright white, oval, and about three inches long.

As a rule, the alligator's nest is made of old leaves, twigs, and grass, mixed with sand and mud. In captivity, if a female is given sand and nothing else, she will make her nest of sand. Whatever is available, she scrapes it together, using her feet and tail, until she has a mound about 18 to 30 inches high and three to five feet across. The job usually takes two or three days, with much of the work done at night, and time out for resting and feeding.

The alligator lays her eggs

When finally the nest is ready, the female digs a large hole in the top. In doing this, she uses first one hind foot and then the other. She places her body over the hole, usually keeping one foot inside it. When her eggs drop into the nest, this foot prevents them from falling on one another hard enough to break. The eggs are bright white, oval, the same size at both ends, and about three inches long.

The average alligator's nest will have about 30 eggs, but the number seems to depend on the size of the female. At the Everglades Wonder Gardens, an eight-foot alligator has been observed to lay 21 eggs, and a nine-foot female to lay 35 eggs, while a 'gator 10 feet long laid 42 eggs. Some females have been known to lay more than 50 eggs.

With all her eggs laid, the female carefully covers them over. To do this, she crawls around the sides of the nest, pushing up material to fill in the hole. She does not crawl directly over the top, where her whole weight would be on the eggs.

Many reptiles simply abandon their eggs, once they are laid. Not so the alligator. Depending on the weather, eggs may take two or even three months to hatch. During this time, the decaying material in the nest keeps them at a steady temperature. All this while the mother 'gator guards her nest. Hour after hour, she will lie with her chin actually resting on it. Now and then, she goes searching for something to eat, but never very far away. Sometimes she lies nearby, hidden in the bushes or the water.

In the wild, raccoons, rats, and many other animals would feast on the alligator eggs if given a chance. They rarely have a chance. Not even a hungry bear wants to take on a mother alligator.

If a man approaches the nest, the female will raise her head, open her mouth, and make a loud, hissing noise. This is clearly meant as a warning, and sounds like it. If the man keeps moving toward the nest, the female 'gator will lunge forward, her mouth wide open. Whether she would actually attack is uncertain. Nobody I know has ever stayed to find out! But I have a friend who spent most of one afternoon up a tree, with the female alligator down below, hissing at him.

In areas where alligators have been heavily hunted and killed for their hides, they learn to be fearful of man — otherwise, they could not live long enough to lay eggs. In such places, the female 'gator will stay near her nest, protecting it from other animals. But she will hide if a man approaches. One naturalist, who had worked only in an area where hunting was permitted, claimed that no alligator would defend her nest against a man. Then he visited the Everglades National Park, where the 'gators are protected. Here he went to examine an alligator nest — and was promptly chased back into his boat.

The 'gator eggs hatch

Shortly before the eggs are ready to hatch, the hard, outer shell begins to crack. Inside this is a much thinner, softer shell that looks as if it were made of plastic. And while it is still inside this shell,

This baby alligator has broken its way through the hard outer shell and the thin inner shell of its egg.

the baby alligator begins to make grunting noises: a sort of "*Uh! Uh! Uh!*" that may be heard 20 or 30 feet away.

Exactly what the mother does at this time is uncertain. Most naturalists believe that she breaks open the nest. Without this help, they say, many of the baby 'gators would die inside, unable to escape. Others claim the mother does not help in any way. Probably the mother does help, at least in some cases.

After breaking through its shells, the baby alligator takes a brief rest before crawling completely out.

A newly-hatched baby alligator will head immediately for the nearest water and start to look for food.

But it is also certain that, when the female has been killed guarding the nest, at least some of the babies will hatch later with no help.

At the tip of the baby 'gator's nose, before it is hatched, there is a tiny, hard bump that comes to a point. This is called a caruncle, or an egg-tooth. Later, this will disappear. But the unhatched 'gator uses it to slit open the soft inner shell of the egg. The hard, outer shell has already cracked. The baby sticks its head out, usually rests there for awhile, then crawls out into the daylight. It is about eight inches long, with teeth like needles. Going *"Uh! Uh! Uh!"* it heads immediately for the nearest body of water, ready to eat. What happens after that is described a little later.

How American Crocodiles Nest and Hatch

The courtship and nesting of the American crocodile — and most other crocodilians — are very much like those of the alligator. But there are some differences.

The crocodile's nest is usually built even closer to the pond or creek bank than is the alligator's. In such places, there may not be either leaves or grass. Instead, the crocodile builds her nest of dirt. In the Everglades, this may be sand or marl, a kind of clay-like earth.

The crocodile nest is not usually as tall as that of the alligator. Most are about a foot and a half or two feet high and seven or eight feet across at the bottom. Sometimes, however, the female crocodile will simply dig a hole in the sand, lay her eggs, and cover them over. Nests of this sort may not be more than a few inches higher than the sand around them.

This crocodile nest, made largely of marl, was built near the bank of a small creek inside Everglades National Park.

Like the alligator, the female crocodile guards her nest. But so many American crocodiles have been killed by hide hunters that few remain. These few have learned to be afraid of man. Although female crocodiles protect their nests from hungry animals, they very rarely try to defend them from men. In recent years, state and federal laws have been passed to protect both alligators and crocodiles. But crocodiles particularly are still very scarce, and very shy.

In the Everglades, government scientists are now working to learn more about crocodiles, in an effort to save them from extermination. One of these men, Dr. John Ogden, has placed recording thermometers inside crocodile nests. He learned that, although the outside temperature varied, the temperature inside the nest stayed the same, day and night. This was usually one or two degrees above 100.

Nests made of marl, and even some made of sand, tend to bake hard under the Florida sun. Dr. Ogden believes it would be impossible for the babies to escape if the mother did not open the nest for them.

At the Everglades Wonder Gardens, the Piper brothers tried for several years to hatch the eggs of

A very young American crocodile hatched at Everglades National Park.

captive crocodiles, but with no success. Sometimes they gave the female sand with which to make her own nest. Sometimes they took the eggs and buried them in a nest of their making. Yet they did not hatch.

The brothers went into the Everglades and, staying quietly hidden, watched the nest of a wild crocodile for several days. Late one evening they saw the female approach her nest, making low, grunting noises. From inside the nest, the babies began to answer. The female then broke open the nest, exposing the eggs. One by one, the babies cut through the soft inner shells, and came grunting into the world.

Since then, the Pipers have been able to hatch crocodile eggs in the Wonder Gardens. They believe the female in captivity loses the impulse to open her nest. Now, when they think the crocodile eggs are ready to hatch, one of the Pipers will crouch down close to the nest and grunt. If the babies answer from inside the eggs, the Pipers break open the nest. If there is no answer, they wait a day or two and try again.

The Young Alligators

To repeat, when baby alligators hatch, they head directly for the nearest body of water, even if that water is several hundred feet away and out of sight. How they know which way to go, no one yet understands — but they do. The baby alligator also knows instinctively how to swim. Born hungry, it plunges into the water and starts looking for something to eat. Tadpoles, water bugs, spiders, anything small enough to swallow is gobbled up.

For a long while naturalists believed that baby alligators stayed with their mother for a year, or even two years, and that she carefully looked after them. Now it seems that this is only partially true. Since the female usually makes her nest close to her home territory, the water that the babies head for is quite likely to be her home. And here they may stay for a year or even two before instinct sends them looking for a place of their own.

Adult alligators will usually tolerate and sometimes protect the baby 'gators. Sometimes an adult may even let the babies sun on its back.

During this time, the mother tolerates them. They may crawl on her back, as if she were a floating log, and sun themselves. They may even share her food under certain conditions. An alligator, male or female, that has killed a pig or some other large animal will often swim about with big chunks of it in its mouth. At such times, young alligators may nibble at the edges. But it is very doubtful that the mother deliberately feeds her babies.

The female will also defend the young. If a young alligator is picked up by a man, or attacked by some animal, it gives a distress call. This is distinctly different from the grunting, *"Uh! Uh!"* It sounds a good bit like the barking of a small puppy. And if the mother hears it, she comes charging.

Strangely, however, it is not the mother alone who will answer this distress call. So will every grown alligator in the area, male as well as female. Exactly why they do this is uncertain. Some naturalists believe that at least some of the adults come hurrying to eat the young 'gator, rather than to help it!

It is true that large alligators sometimes eat small ones. But this happens rarely, quite possibly only in times of near-starvation. Most of the animals that might eat a baby alligator could, in turn, be eaten by a big alligator. In answering a baby's distress call, the big 'gators may simply be hoping to make a meal of the baby's enemy, not the baby. Or they may be truly trying to help.

Even with such help, baby 'gators lead dangerous lives. For them, there is no really safe place. Much of their own feeding is done in the shallow water at the edge of the pond or creek. And here the raccoons and bobcats stalk their own food, which includes baby 'gators. Big wading birds such as the blue heron, the great white heron, and the American egret, stand motionless in the shallows, ready to strike with knife-like beaks. Hungry snakes move silently through the tall grasses and shallow water. Even bullfrogs that don't look to be as big as the baby alligators will sometimes feed on them. And if the small 'gators seek safety in deep water, the large bass and garfish may be waiting for them. Some scientists believe that not more than one baby alligator out of 100 lives to be three years old.

The first few years

If the young alligator does manage to escape its enemies, it will grow about one foot a year. And as it grows, it hunts for bigger food. It eats crawfish and shrimps, lesser water snakes and crabs. It catches small fish and frogs, including the bullfrogs that not so long before were able to feed on it.

As the days grow short and the weather turns cool in late autumn, all alligators become sluggish. Those that live in the northern part of their range — Georgia, Louisiana, almost anywhere except the southern

A young alligator may defend itself with vigor. A Florida wildlife officer, banding young alligators, found that every time he put his boot near this one, it leaped to attack.

part of Florida — lose their appetites. The adults will dig or find a cave of some sort, and here they may lie motionless for days or even weeks, depending on the weather. If young 'gators are still sharing a pond with their mother, they probably also share her cave. Now and then on warm days, they may all come out to feed or bask in the sun, then go back to the cave.

With early spring, the alligators are on the move again. The young feed hungrily to keep growing. By late July or August, new eggs hatch and a new brood

49

of babies may move into the pool with the adult female and her young of one or two years before. But as the number of alligators in one area grows larger, the food supply for each naturally gets smaller. So about this time the two-year-olds generally set out to find a place of their own.

By the age of four, the young alligator is about four feet in length. It is no longer afraid of wading birds, raccoons, or even bobcats. Indeed, there is almost nothing in the wild that it does fear. And at this time an odd thing happens. The voice changes. No longer will the young alligator go, *"Uh! Uh! Uh!"* No longer will it make the distress call. Instead, both the male and female begin to practice a bellow. This is a little uncertain at first, but soon gets deeper and louder.

The Full-grown 'Gator

When the young alligator goes off on its own, it may spend a year or more simply wandering about, with no particular home. Nobody knows very much about its actions at this period in its life. But about the time it starts to bellow, apparently feeling grown up, it may set up housekeeping on its own.

Alligator homes

The type of home the alligator makes for itself depends largely on the area, of course. If the 'gator's home is in a river or creek, it may dig a kind of cave in the bank. Actually, most of this "digging" is done by pushing its long snout into the soft mud of the bank while swishing its powerful tail back and forth. This not only forces a hole into the bank, it also washes away the mud. Gradually, the cave gets bigger until it extends well back under the river bank. It may have bends along the way, to avoid rocks and

This alligator's body blends so perfectly with the reeds, it is difficult to see.

tree roots. At the far end, there is a room large enough for the alligator to turn around in. If the alligator's home is in a pond or swamp, it will make a different kind of den. And in southern Florida, particularly in the Everglades, this kind of den is almost as important to other animals as it is to the alligator. In fact, without the alligator, vast parts of the Everglades might turn into lifeless desert. Here is the reason for this.

When the alligator makes its home in a shallow pond, it will dig a basin, usually in the deepest part. To do this, the 'gator swings its tail back and forth, scraping away the earth, the weeds, and water plants that grew there. With its armored body, it pushes all this material into a low, circular wall. As long as the alligator lives in this spot, it will keep the center part of its den clean, uprooting any new weeds and water plants that start to grow. But on the rim around the home basin water lilies, cattails, pickerelweed, and other plants grow thickly.

'Gator holes

Sometimes the alligator will make its home where there is no natural pond at all. Then the 'gator digs away the soft, swampy earth to make its own pond. Here too the center is kept clean. And here too water plants grow lushly around the rim.

Dens of this sort are called "'gator holes." Normally, they hold water the year around. And in the usually mild winters of southern Florida, this water is enough to protect the 'gator, even on the coldest days.

But 'gator holes do much more than protect the alligators which made them. In southern Florida, there are usually heavy rains during the summer. Then in the winter and early spring there is a long period of drought. At this time, most shallow ponds dry up. Where there had been swamp during the summer, the land becomes so dry it may crack like a broken plate. In many parts of the Everglades, the 'gator holes may hold the only water available within several miles.

Without these holes, there would be a great loss of animal life. To them come the small Everglades deer to drink. Here come the bobcats, the raccoons, the otters. Snakes move softly through the plants growing about the rim of the hole. Frogs and insects live here. And here come the water birds of the Everglades, herons and egrets and ibis and spoonbills. They feed on the frogs and insects and small fish, as well as drink the water.

Without these 'gator holes, some of the animals might be able to leave and find water elsewhere. Many, however, would simply die.

Certainly, the tiny fish that gather in the holes would die. And to man this is tremendously important. When the summer rains come, the 'gator holes fill and overflow. In little trickles and streams the water spreads across the surrounding country. With it go the tiny fish, into the newly-formed ponds and swamps. Here they feed on the vast hordes of mosquito larvae just beginning to hatch with the spreading wetness. And so the alligator functions as a vital part of nature's mosquito control.

How 'gators help birds

Odd as it may seem, alligators are also important in the conservation of bird life in another way besides the food and drink provided by their 'gator holes. True, hungry 'gators will gobble down any duck or wading bird they are able to catch. But they save far more birds than they destroy. It happens this way.

The alligator will, of course, eat the coot in the water if it gets a chance, but actually alligators are important in the conservation of bird life.

Where there are alligators, there may also be large rookeries of nesting water birds. These are frequently located in swampy areas where the herons and egrets and ibis may nest by the tens of thousands. Rats, raccoons, snakes, and bobcats gather around, hoping to feast on the eggs and on the young birds. The parent birds defend their nests as best they can, but these animals are capable of climbing the low trees and driving away the parents.

The alligators cannot climb the trees. Instead, they lie motionless as logs on the ground beneath. Of course, they may eat any young bird that falls out of its nest, but chances are it would die anyway. Beneath a rookery, the alligators will feed chiefly on the prowling rats, raccoons, and snakes. And so, without intending to, they save the lives of countless birds.

Growth and food

As an alligator gets older, it grows more and more slowly. By the time the male 'gator is 20 to 30 years old and 15 to 16 feet long, it will probably quit growing altogether. Most females stop growing at about 10 feet.

Although a very old alligator may have almost no teeth left, it will still have powerful jaws. And since its teeth were not made for chewing, but for gripping

Lying motionless in the water, with only its snout, eyes, and a bit of the back showing, an alligator may look like a half-sunken log.

and tearing and holding, even the old alligator seems to get along very well. It feeds chiefly on fish, snakes, turtles, wading birds — anything it can catch and swallow whole.

Large alligators have been known to kill dogs, pigs, and very rarely, animals as big as a deer or cow. This is done in an odd manner. A hunting alligator may lie motionless, almost hidden in the shallow water near the bank of its pond or river. A cow coming to drink may not see it, or may mistake it for a half-sunken log. As the cow lowers her head, the alligator lunges with incredible speed. It catches the cow by the nose, or possibly by the leg. With powerful sweeps of its tail, the alligator begins to roll over and over, at the same time backing into deeper water. So violent is this spinning motion, and so powerful is the grip of the alligator's jaws, that the cow's leg or head may be torn completely off the body.

In captivity, alligators frequently crowd together when they are being fed. Then one 'gator may clamp his huge jaws upon another alligator's foot, mistaking it for a fish. If the gripping alligator starts to roll, the other alligator must roll with it — or have its foot torn completely off.

There is no doubt that alligators do feel pain at such times. Yet the pain seems to end very quickly. The mutilated foot heals rapidly, and the injured 'gator appears to get along as well as before.

Men who work with alligators sometimes make good use of this reptile's curious habit of rolling over and over when fighting. Bill and Lester Piper were once called on to capture a 12-foot 'gator that had, somehow, wandered into a nearby town. They flipped a lasso over the 'gator's head and jerked it tight. Immediately, the alligator started to roll — and so wrapped the rope round and round itself until it was tied down from end to end.

Does the alligator use its tail as a weapon?

People disagree about the answer to this question. According to some of the old folktales, the alligator's tail is actually more dangerous than its jaws. Many stories tell how an alligator may strike a deer or other large animal with its tail and knock it down. Only then, the stories say, does the 'gator seize its prey with its mouth and drag it into the water.

A few naturalists laugh at these stories. One man wrote that it's as silly to think an alligator fights with its tail as it is to say that a lion charges rear-end first toward its prey! The truth seems to be somewhere in-between. Certainly, an alligator's jaws are its chief weapon. The jaws catch and crush its prey. But the tail does sometimes play an important role in the outcome. Whether this is a regular part of the 'gator's offensive action or whether it happens by chance is still to be proved.

When an alligator turns toward food or an enemy on its right or left, the 'gator's head does not move in one direction and its tail in the other. Instead, the two swing toward one another so the alligator's body will almost form a circle. If the thing the alligator is

When an alligator turns quickly, the head and tail move toward one another, almost forming a circle. Any small animal that is near the reptile's tail will be knocked toward its jaws.

attacking is near its tail, the tail may strike it first, and this will knock the object *toward* the alligator's gaping jaws.

Many people have described how an alligator, swimming into a school of fish, will swirl suddenly, the tail knocking fish toward the head. Bill Piper once watched an alligator lie motionless in the grass as a chicken approached. The chicken apparently mistook the 'gator for a log and pecked at something on its tail. Instantly, the 'gator struck. The tail knocked the chicken high in the air, and the jaws seized it before it fell.

Is the Alligator
Dangerous to Man?

In the summer of 1969, a farmer named Carl Standridge was plowing with a tractor in the Ocala National Forest in Florida. As he passed the edge of a marsh, a nine-foot alligator rushed out. Its stubby legs holding the body clear of the ground, head lifted, jaws open, it moved with amazing speed straight at the tractor.

Startled, Mr. Standridge swerved the tractor away from the attacker, Still charging, the 'gator clamped its teeth on the rear of the tractor, and held on. With the reptile dragging behind, Standridge drove to his nearby home. He believed the alligator had in some way become fastened to the tractor and couldn't let go, so he got down to investigate.

Instantly, the alligator let go the tractor and started for the man. But it was slower-moving now, and Standridge outran it to his front door. From inside his house, he telephoned Ross Allen at the Reptile Institute at Silver Springs.

When Allen and an assistant arrived, the alligator was still in Mr. Standridge's front yard. Promptly, it turned on them. Having come prepared, one man held it off with the long pole while the other threw a lasso over its head and tied the jaws together. It was then taken to the Reptile Institute and put in a pen. It is still there. It is also still mean-tempered, ready to fight anything that comes near, whether it is a man or another alligator.

"In more than 40 years of working with alligators," Ross Allen says now, "this was the first and only time I ever knew of one attacking a man without cause. This one is a male, so it was not defending a nest. What caused its strange behavior and why it is so mean-tempered, I have no idea."

Normally, there are only two reasons why an alligator would attack man or any other creature. One of these is hunger. The alligator plans to eat the thing it attacks. The other reason is defense. This might be in defense of itself, in defense of its nest or home territory, or in answer to the distress call of the young.

Nobody can say surely just how an alligator judges what it can or cannot eat. Many naturalists believe that the alligator judges largely by the height of the creature rather than the bulk. In connection with this, they point out that there is no known case (aside from that of Farmer Standridge) where an alligator has attacked a standing man, except in defense. An alligator will lunge at a man in defense of its nest. But it does not chase him. If the man leaves the alligator's territory alone, the alligator will leave the man alone.

On the other hand, alligators have been known to attack small children playing near the edge of a pond or river. On a very few occasions, alligators have attacked men or women while swimming. In 1952, an alligator grabbed a nine-year-old girl who was fishing in a southern Florida pond. As the 'gator dragged her toward deep water, a 10-year-old boy, fishing nearby, rushed to help. He beat so fiercely at the alligator's head with his fists that the creature released the girl, and the boy pulled her to safety. Later, President Harry Truman gave the boy a well-deserved award for his bravery.

In captivity, alligators become accustomed to being fed. When the keeper throws them fish, the reptiles rush forward to eat, without examining too closely what it is they are eating. This same thing may happen in parks or in ponds where alligators have become semi-tame. Visitors throw them marsh-

Alligators in captivity have learned to lunge out of the water like porpoises to catch tidbits of food.

mallows — for some strange reason, alligators *love* marshmallows — or bits of sandwiches. In such a place, if a child fell into the water, the alligators might seize it. This would not be because they are naturally man-eaters but because they have learned to believe that anything thrown to them was meant to be eaten.

In Florida, the American crocodile is far more shy than the alligator. There is only one known case of a Florida crocodile killing a man. This happened many years ago when hunters shot a crocodile on a river bank. Believing it dead, one of the hunters went close and kicked the reptile. Instantly, the crocodile whirled and grabbed the man by the waist. The other hunters killed the crocodile and rescued the man, but he died of his injuries.

It is quite possible that, long ago, alligators may have been more dangerous than they are today. For one thing, there were vast numbers of them. Nor had they yet learned to be so afraid of man. William Bartram, while paddling a small boat through a part of Florida where few white men had ever been, found that sometimes the 'gators were not afraid at all.

"The alligators," Bartram wrote, "gathered around my harbor from all quarters." But he was determined to get past them to a place where he wanted to fish. "Ere I had half way reached the place, I was attacked on all sides, several endeavoring to overset the canoe . . . two very large ones attacked me closely, at the same instant, rushing up with their heads and part of their bodies above the water. . . ."

At this time, Bartram was sitting down in a small boat. The hungry alligators had been feeding on fish and possibly mistook Bartram and his canoe for some overgrown mullet. Even so, he was able to keep them off with a club. And when he paddled his boat close to shore, the alligators "drew off and kept aloof."

There is now one excellent rule on how to behave if you see an alligator or crocodile in the wild. Leave it alone. If it should move toward you, which is highly unlikely, then you have probably come close to its nest. Back off. To repeat, leave the alligator alone — and it will leave you alone.

Alligator wrestling

In Florida, there are a number of roadside shows in which men wrestle with live alligators. Several of these are operated by Seminole Indians. In some, the man goes into a pen and wrestles the alligator on land. In others, the alligator is put into a deep pool, the man dives in and wrestles the alligator under-

A Seminole Indian alligator wrestler produces an excellent view of the inside of this reptile's mouth.

water. The show ends when the man drags the alligator onto land, rolls it on its back, and rubs its belly. At this point, the alligator (as has been described earlier) either goes to sleep or becomes unconscious.

There are several reasons why a skillful man may defeat an alligator, even though the alligator may be far more powerful in many ways. An alligator's reactions are determined by instinct rather than reason. If a man invades the alligator's territory — its pen or its pool — the alligator may open its jaws and make a loud, hissing noise. But, well-fed and sluggish, it really just wants to be left alone.

The muscles with which an alligator closes its jaws are extremely powerful. Strangely, however, the muscles with which it opens its jaws are quite weak. Also, these are located at the back, where the jaw is hinged. If a friend grasps two of your fingers near the end, he can hold them together without difficulty.

Alligator wrestling at the Ross Allen Reptile Institute, Silver Springs, Florida.

But if he catches them back near the hand, then it will be much more difficult to hold them. It is the same way with an alligator. If a man catches the 'gator's snout near the tip, he can hold the jaws together with one hand.

An alligator wrestler, then, usually jumps astride the alligator's back. In this position, he cannot be hit by the tail or bitten. Then, with one hand, he clutches the tip of the alligator's snout — only when it is already closed, of course — and holds it shut.

Although powerful, alligators tire very quickly. The man needs only hold on until the 'gator wears itself out. Also, the alligators used in these shows may have been wrestled many times before. They know how the act is going to come out, and all they want is to get it over and go back to sleep.

Alligator wrestling is chiefly a stunt. But it is a stunt requiring skill and strength. And a slip might mean the loss of several fingers or a hand.

The Nile Crocodile

Two thousand years before the Spanish conquistadors saw their first American alligator, Egyptians were well acquainted with the Nile crocodile. Indeed, ancient man and the Nile crocodile were living close together before the dawn of recorded history. It was the Nile crocodile around which most of the legends about crocodilians arose.

A crocodile often rests with its mouth open. It may lie like this, motionless, for a half hour or more. And some four hundred years before Christ, Herodotus, a Greek historian, tried to explain why. The Nile crocodile, Herodotus wrote, kept its mouth open to attract insects. These swarmed in, and when, finally, the crocodile had its mouth full — *chomp!* Its jaws closed, and it ate them.

But this was not all the story, according to Herodotus. There was also a vicious little beast called an ichneumon. This would sneak up on the open-

A crocodile will rest for long periods with its mouth open. Some naturalists believe that fresh air and sunshine prevent the growth of fungus in the mouth.

mouthed crocodile, leap down its throat, and eat the crocodile from inside out!

Today, the story is largely forgotten. But naturalists still puzzle over why crocodiles rest with their mouths open.

When a crocodile or an alligator senses danger, it will open its mouth and hiss. This, with the gaping jaws and the long teeth, acts as a warning. But when the danger is removed, the alligator shuts its mouth. Some naturalists believe the crocodile simply forgets to shut its mouth and so continues to lie with it open. Many naturalists, however, declare the crocodile opens its mouth whether or not there is danger. They believe that, by leaving its mouth open to sun and fresh air, the crocodile prevents the growth of fungus that might otherwise develop.

Some of the ancient Egyptians worshipped crocodiles as gods. Crocodile bodies were sometimes mummified along with those of the Pharaohs and buried in the pyramids. In at least one place, human sacrifices were offered to sacred crocodiles kept in a pool. This was supposed to prevent the Nile River from flooding and drowning the people.

One Egyptian magician is reported to have had a trained crocodile. It went around eating the people the magician didn't like. It is true that the Nile crocodiles, which may grow to be 16 or possibly 17 feet long, are more vicious than the American crocodiles or alligators. They have often attacked children and even adults bathing in African rivers. But anyone who could train a crocodile to go hunting for a particular person like a bloodhound must have been a magician indeed.

The Nile crocodile is not confined to the Nile River. It has been found over almost all of Africa — except, of course, in the deserts and high mountains. And although some of them have eaten people, the people more often have eaten the crocodiles. In early times, the natives hunted the crocodiles with spears and clubs. Whole villages might go on such a hunt. When a crocodile was killed, it was often torn apart on the spot and the meat eaten raw. This was sup-

A crocodile, captured at the Nairobi Dam, is being transferred to the Nairobi National Park.

posed to give the person who ate it the strength of a crocodile.

Nesting and caring for eggs

The Nile crocodile, like its American relative, digs its nest near the bank of a river. The hole is about two feet deep and there are usually 50 to 60 eggs in each. These are covered with about one foot of sand.

Depending on the weather, the eggs take about 90 days to hatch. During all this time the female guards her nest carefully, rarely leaving it even to

73

eat. This is particularly important because of the great number of animals that would feast on the eggs if given a chance. Baboons, hyenas, many kinds of birds, and huge lizards called monitors prowl endlessly around the nesting places, waiting for a chance to feed.

In the Uganda National Park, boats loaded with visitors sometimes pass close to where the crocodiles are nesting. Then the female crocodiles, grown fearful of man, may slip away into the river. The baboons, monitors, and hyenas, which are rarely hunted and less afraid of man, promptly rush out and start digging up the eggs.

Game wardens now try to keep visitors away from the nesting areas. But some people find it exciting to watch animals raiding the crocodile nests. Sometimes they see a female crocodile, overcoming her own fear of man, rush out to chase away the baboons and monitors. So the boats keep coming — and each year a larger part of the nests are destroyed.

When the crocodile eggs hatch

When the babies of the Nile crocodile hatch, they do not head immediately for water, each one on its own, as do alligators. Instead, they seem to head for the shade of their mother's body. If they have been uncovered by man and the mother is not there, they may crawl to a nearby log and lie beside it. One naturalist uncovered a nest of crocodile eggs, then lay down beside it. The hatchlings, grunting softly, crawled to lie beside him.

The life of the young Nile crocodile is even more dangerous than that of the alligator, so the mother's protection is very important. When the young are hatched, she leads them away from the river and into some marshy area with high grass. Here there is a better chance of hiding from the animals that might otherwise feed on them.

Baby crocodiles at a game reserve in Rhodesia.

Enemies of the Nile crocodile

Once the crocodile has grown to be five or six feet long, however, it has little to fear except man. The lion is supposed to be the king of the jungle, but not even a lion would want to tangle with a full-grown crocodile. The one animal from which a big crocodile might well retreat is the hippopotamus. Hippos often go wading in the rivers and lakes where crocodiles make their homes. And here adult crocodiles have been known to eat baby hippos. But the female hippos, protecting their young, have also been known to trample adult crocodiles to death.

It is probable that crocodiles and elephants rarely tangle with one another. But an African explorer once saw such a battle. The elephant was drinking water from a stream. The crocodile probably saw the elephant's trunk and nothing else. Anyway, the crocodile grabbed the trunk in its jaws and began to whirl, trying to pull the elephant into the river. Instead, the elephant pulled the crocodile onto land. Then, stamping with all four feet, it crushed the crocodile to death.

The Saltwater Crocodile

The saltwater crocodile gets its name from the fact that it is the most seagoing of all the crocodilians. It may be found from western India to northern Australia, and north through all the East Indies to the Philippines. It has been seen 100 miles or more at sea, swimming steadily along with sweeps of its powerful tail. Several years ago, one came crawling out of the sea on an island 600 miles from any other land.

Usually, however, these crocodiles are found in shallow bays and inlets of the sea, so they are often called estuarian crocodiles. Some members of the family, however, don't live in salt water at all, but may spend their lives in rivers and lakes. Growing to a gigantic 19 or 20 feet in length, the saltwater crocodile is the most aggressive and dangerous to man of all the crocodilians.

Throughout much of its range, the saltwater croc-

This crocodile is ten feet long. Imagine one twenty feet in length.

odile was not heavily hunted until recent years. Nor were there any hippos, elephants, or other animals big enough to cause it trouble in its home territory. Instead, a full-grown crocodile could kill and eat just about anything it found. As a result, some big saltwater crocodiles will rush toward any loud splashing noise they hear, ready to attack.

Wilfred Neill, an American naturalist working in New Guinea, witnessed such an attack. Two natives in a dugout canoe were hunting turtles in a lake. One of the men paddled while the other stood in the bow with a spear. As the craft moved through water lilies, a huge saltwater crocodile lying motionless nearby heard it. Instantly, the reptile charged. Lunging half out of the water, it caught the spearman by an ankle, at the same time overturning the canoe.

With its jaws clamped on the native's ankle, the crocodile began to whirl. The man tried desperately to roll with it. The second man, who had been paddling, quickly caught up a floating spear and stabbed the crocodile. The creature released its victim and both men escaped. But the man who had been bitten lost his foot.

Almost any animal, including very small alligators, may fight if cornered. But the young saltwater crocodile is particularly savage. Naturalists trying to collect them for study have referred to them as "fiendish little brutes," and "positively the most vicious of reptiles."

While studying saltwater crocodiles in New Guinea, Wilfred Neill found two piles of *kunai* grass that he thought were nests. Keeping a careful eye out for the females, he dug into them. But instead of eggs, he found a freshly killed pig under each mound. Since crocodile tracks led to and from the mounds, Neill felt sure they had been made by crocodiles. But why?

Another naturalist in New Guinea found a far more unusual mound. Traveling through the jungle with a group of natives, they heard what sounded like a human voice, calling out in pain. On investigating, they found a badly wounded man lying under a pile of grass. The man told them that he had been attacked by a saltwater crocodile which had dragged him to this spot. Apparently believing the man was dead, the crocodile covered him over with grass and left.

It would seem from this that, when a saltwater crocodile kills an animal too large to eat at once, it buries its prey under a pile of grass. But does it come back to feed after the body has partially decayed and may easily be torn apart? No one knows for sure.

The saltwater crocodile, like the alligator, can roar —a long, wavering boom. Yet, despite its size, it can't match the tremendous bellow of the alligator.

A crocodile in South Africa.

Caimans

Caimans may be found over a vast area of tropical South America, Central America, and southern Mexico. There are five species. These are commonly called the black caiman, the broad-nosed caiman, the smooth-fronted caiman, the dwarf caiman, and the spectacled caiman. The spectacled caimans are sometimes divided into four subspecies.

All caimans are very much like alligators, to whom they are closely related. They are also very much like one another — although sometimes they differ in rather curious ways.

Like alligators, all the caimans build their nests of leaves and grass, scraped together with a little dirt. The females defend their nests. The larger and more powerful species will even defend them against man; the smaller species will defend them against any animal they are capable of driving away. The babies grunt and have a distress call much like that of baby alligators. Their cry, however, is a little higher and more birdlike — a very curious sound to come from what looks like a lizard. What part, if any, the mother plays in raising her young is unknown.

The black is the largest of all the caimans, sometimes reaching a length of 15 feet. It lives in the Amazon River basin, and many of the Indian natives fear it. Like the saltwater crocodile, it sometimes dashes toward a splashing in the water before it knows who or what is there, and it might attack a small child. The black caiman lives chiefly in shallow water, around the edges of lakes or near the banks of rivers. Lifting its body clear of the bottom, it can charge through this shallow water with surprising speed.

The black caiman hunts mostly at night, and it has excellent eyesight, even in the dark. This was proved one night by an experiment conducted by Ross Allen's Reptile Institute. Standing in the dark, a man waved his hand above a pen containing several species of crocodilians. The lone black caiman swung around to watch, although no other animal moved.

As its name implies, the dwarf is the smallest of the caimans. It rarely grows to be more than four feet long. Like the alligator, it may make or find a cave with an underwater entrance. But, since the weather never gets cold where the dwarf caiman lives, it does not use this to hibernate. Instead, it seems to sleep there during the daytime, then come out at night to feed.

The spectacled are the most common and widespread type of the caimans. They are found over a large part of South and Central America. As mentioned before, baby spectacled caimans are often sold in pet shops and called "alligators."

The younger the animal, the brighter the markings on its body. Above, a caiman; below, an alligator.

Where two or more species of caiman inhabit the same general area, what scientists call an "ecological separation" is in effect. One species may prefer to feed around rocks and rapidly moving water. Another may live only a short distance away but where the water is calm or slow moving. Or one species may prefer a heavily shaded swamp, while a neighboring species basks in the sunlit waters just beyond the

Crocodilians have five toes on the front feet and four on the back. This young caiman has a toe missing on its left forefoot.

trees. In this way, those with differing habits do not need to fight one another for food and both colonies may survive.

There are no hippopotamuses or elephants in the South American jungles, but the caiman does have one dangerous enemy there besides man. This is the anaconda, a giant snake that grows to be more than 20 feet in length. These creatures will feed not only on the dwarf caiman, but on adult black caiman seven feet or more in length. The anaconda, like the boa constrictor, kills its prey by crushing the victim in its coils. There is no record of anyone having watched a battle between an anaconda and a crocodile, but anacondas have been found with large, freshly-killed crocodiles inside them.

The Gavial

Not many people think of either the alligator or the crocodile as a handsome creature — unless they compare it with a gavial! Certainly the gavial, with its nose like a broom handle, is the oddest looking of all the crocodilians. But it does have one attractive feature. Its eyes are a soft olive-green, very pretty and different from the eyes of any other crocodilian.

The gavial is found in India, Burma, and in some parts of Borneo. Its amazingly long, slender snout may look grotesque, but for the gavial it is very effective. Gavials feed chiefly on fish, and this perfectly stream-lined snout can slash through the water with terrific speed. At Ross Allen's Reptile Institute, a gavial was placed in a pool of water along with a number of small fish. The fish swam round and round at one end of the pool. For a few moments the gavial lay quietly on the bottom at the other end. Then, very slowly, it crept forward. It moved so slowly the fish did not notice. Also, it did not come directly toward the fish but just to one side. When it was close to its prey, its

The gavial's long snout is used in catching fish.

snout lashed sideways. The movement was so fast that watchers saw only a blur, but the gavial had several fish clamped in its jaws. After that, whenever the gavial struck at the fish, it rarely missed.

Except for catching fish, the gavial tends to be quite shy and retiring. There are no known records of it actually attacking a man. Even so, it has acquired something of a bad reputation. This is easy to understand. The gavial is not only ugly, it also may be the longest of all the crocodilians. There are stories about gavials 30 feet long or more. Of course, there are stories about alligators and crocodiles of this size as well, but with no proof at all. Nor are there any actual records of a gavial 30 feet long. But there are authentic records of gavials slightly more than 21 feet long — and that would look like 30 to most people!

Among the natives of India there are many stories about gavials eating people. Probably most of these got started when some dead gavial was opened and found to contain rings, bracelets, and other bits of jewelry. But if a gavial did actually eat a person, then almost certainly the person was already dead. In India, according to custom, human corpses are sometimes thrown into the rivers, rather than being cremated or buried. It is possible that a gavial might eat part of a drifting body.

There is another and even more probable reason why gavials might sometimes contain bracelets and other bits of jewelry. Since corpses have been thrown into the rivers of India for hundreds of years, many still adorned with the jewelry they had worn in life, the bottoms of these rivers must be littered with bits of jewelry. And gavials, like the other crocodilians, will swallow rocks, lumps of wood, and other hard objects. The jewelry in a gavial's stomach may have been swallowed to help him digest fish, not as part of a human meal.

Although gavials and the Indian people have lived close together for several thousand years, there has been very little scientific study made of them. It is uncertain what kinds of nests they make and how they care for their young.

The Future of Crocodilians

The age of the dinosaurs, the pterodactyls, the gigantic crocodilians — the Ruling Reptiles — came to an end some 63 million years ago. But those crocodilians that remained continued to rule their private worlds for eons and eons. Even after man appeared on the scene, he troubled the crocodilians very little. Sometimes he hunted them for food, but his weapons were crude. Other animals were easier and less dangerous to kill. In their swamps and along the river banks, the crocodiles and alligators more than held their own.

Eventually, in a relatively few places, man began to drain the crocodilians' swamps to plant farms and build houses. The reptiles pulled back, only slightly troubled. More than enough room remained.

It is only in the present century, a half drop in the oceans of time, that the crocodilians have been threatened with complete extermination as, more and

An unusual head-on view of an American crocodile.

more, man moved into their territory. Swamps were
drained. Along the rivers of South America, some rain
forests were cut down for timber. New industries
polluted the streams.

Still, in the United States there were the Florida
Everglades, and the swamplands of southern Georgia
and Louisiana. Plenty of room for plenty of alligators
— or so it seemed. In other parts of the world there
also remained vast areas where the crocodilians
appeared secure.

No one knows just when man first realized that
hides taken from the bellies of crocodilians, particu-

larly those of the alligator and the saltwater crocodile, could be made into valuable leather. But after World War II this leather became highly popular. Within a few years, the price of hides increased from a few cents a foot to more than six dollars a foot. In Florida, a skilled alligator hunter could make $400 in one night. In Borneo, in the jungles of South and Central America, hide buyers furnished the natives with guns and ammunition. Throughout the tropics of the world, crocodilians were killed by the thousands and tens of thousands.

In many places, the crocodilians inhabited land that was of little or no value. It could not be farmed or built on. No other animals of value lived there. When carefully harvested, crocodiles could be a "crop" of great value to the natives, but not if they were totally destroyed at once. This would be like a farmer who ate all his corn and saved none for planting. There would be no crop to harvest the next year.

Realizing that the species were endangered to the point of extermination, the United States and many other countries passed laws to protect the crocodilians. Unfortunately, in many places these laws are of little value. Poachers continue to kill the giant reptiles. The lands where they might live are being drained and ruined. Truly, the last of the Ruling

Reptiles is in serious danger of disappearing from the earth. Man, not nature, is destroying them. And if man is to save them, then he must know more about their lives and needs than he does at present.

Just how important is it for the female crocodilian to break open her nest when the eggs begin to hatch, and why does she sometimes fail to do this?

Why do all crocodilians swallow rocks and other hard objects? Does this curious custom help or harm them?

In trying to learn more about alligators and protect them, Florida wildlife officers capture young ones in the wild, measure and tag and then release them.

How does a baby alligator, newly hatched from its shell, find its way directly toward water?

Why do crocodiles bask in the sun with their mouths open? Does this actually help to prevent disease?

Naturalists still have no answers for these and many other questions that may be vital. They are questions for the naturalists of the future, for the young people now in school, to try to answer. And these problems must be solved or one more form of animal life may disappear forever.

Index